THE
ELEVENTH
MAN

Memories of the German
Death March, Winter 1945

Thank you
Robert H. Honeycutt
+ Jane Littlejohn

By

Robert H. Honeycutt

&

Jane Littlejohn

THE
ELEVENTH
MAN

Library of Congress Control Number: 2004105089
ISBN 0-9753894-0-8

Printed in the United States of America
First Edition 2004

Published by
Combine Press
Chattanooga, TN

Produced by
PPC Books
Redington Shores, FL

DEDICATION

This book is dedicated to two angels in my life.

To my wife Hazel, whose faith in me all these years has kept me going.

To Jane, who made the dream of this book a reality.

TABLE OF CONTENTS

Introduction

In my years of nursing, I have encountered the human experience of pain and suffering in many forms. As in all great tragedies, there is usually a golden stream running through its core, which is humanity at its best. I believe there is something divine about it; light piercing darkness, beauty for ashes, music in the night. Greater minds than mine have attempted to explain it throughout the centuries, but it is a phenomenon I have witnessed repeatedly in working with people whose lives have been devastated by a cancer diagnosis. There is an emergence of a will to survive, along with amazing courage and grace that transcends ordinary living.

We all heard about it in the September 11th aftermath. Reports emerged of people helping people in dramatic ways, strangers risking their lives for one another. Even now, as war rages in the Middle East and soldiers and civilians on both sides are killed almost daily, there are good and valiant and true deeds occurring that we will never hear about on the news or in history books. These experiences will be told one day to children and grandchildren, to friends and neighbors, in the form of stories.

One of the great privileges of being a nurse has been to be at the bedside (as opposed to the fireside) as these stories are told. I have heard many, and have been especially touched by those who were in World War II. I am told we are losing these veterans now at a rate of about fifteen hundred

per day, and their stories go with them. It is often due to pain and suffering that the stories finally emerge, pure and unrestrained. Unexpectedly. To be present when it happens is a gift.

I was teaching first year nursing students in their first clinical rotation, which is always an interesting challenge. They are especially nervous about entering patient's rooms where they are expected to give baths or shots when they have never done it before on a real patient, so a bit of handholding is required. I was in such a role, helping a student give "the patient" a bath, when this story began to unfold.

"I'm going to beat this cancer, I'm going to beat it," said the elderly man in hospital gown.

"I was shot out of a plane, I walked miles in the snow for days; this cancer isn't going to get me."

"When was this?" I asked.

He went on in a torrent of words that I could not keep up with: bombers, snow, guns, marching, camps. He began to weep.

"What is it you're remembering right now that is making you cry?" I asked.

"All the death. All the death," he sobbed.

"I want to hear your story, but right now you need to rest," I said trying to calm him down.

"I'll come back tomorrow and we'll talk."

When I came back the next day he was gone.

Six months later I was beginning a new job developing a cancer resource center and support program for cancer patients at the same hospital. I was talking with a man and his wife about his colon cancer and nutritional difficulties when something about the man's voice sounded familiar to me. He was dressed in "street clothes" and I did not recognize his face or name.

"Were you in World War II?"

"Yes, I was."

"Were you a POW?"

"Yes, I was."

"Did you have to march in the snow?"

It was him, only he did not remember our previous conversation or meeting me at all. He had been delirious with a widespread infection due to complications of chemotherapy. On the day I last saw him he had been transferred to the ICU, and had come perilously close to the edge of death. As it turned out, I was being introduced to a man who has been there and back many times. He is a survivor, in every sense of the word.

This book is the result of many conversations taking place over almost two years, usually in my living room on Sunday afternoons. One day he brought to my office a hand-written manuscript that he had been writing and weeping over for days. He said, "I have waited almost sixty years to get this off my chest."

This is his story, in his own words.

Jane Littlejohn

PeeWee

I was born in Bessemer, Alabama on June 2, 1923. We moved to South Chattanooga when I was three years old during what is now known as The Great Depression. There was no money then; at least we did not have much. There were nine kids in our family, seven boys and two girls, and there was many a night we went to bed hungry. I was the sixth child. The oldest was my sister, Lillie, (she always called me Tootsie) then four brothers, Wesley, Harry, Edward, and Walter (Bug). The younger ones were Milton (Shang), Christine, and Raymond.

My dad was a painter and wallpaper hanger and he didn't make much money and what he did make never made it home. He was an alcoholic and would come home roaring drunk after spending his paycheck on bootleg whiskey. There were some rough scenes when he came home to my mother and we sometimes got caught in the middle of it. Mom's life was one of taking care of nine kids and having to move just about every time the rent came due. But we had to eat and we all found ways to help, even the kids.

When I was about eight years old, my brother, Edward, and I sold peanuts and apples and candy to help make a living for our family. We would go around together so I would not get lost, and I would go into the businesses and sell my peanuts and snacks to the employees.

I also worked at a meat market on Broad St., called Roberts Market. Everyone called me PeeWee because I was so little. I would take a coaster wagon to deliver food to the customers by myself. I remember eggs were eight cents a dozen and gasoline was thirteen cents a gallon. I worked for fifteen cents an hour and was lucky to get that. We had a patch of ground behind our house where I raised a small garden to have food to sell or eat. I was PeeWee, a little kid trying to help feed a family of eleven. I guess the depression first taught me about surviving. I didn't know anything else.

I went to Third District School in South Chattanooga. A lot of times I didn't have any shoes to go so I went barefooted. I made it to the seventh grade. I kept working, learning how to paint and hang wallpaper with my Dad, and also was good at construction. These were skills that would stick with me the rest of my life.

The South side of Chattanooga was pretty rough and there were racial tensions. We were all in what you might call gangs, but the most damage we did was a rumble at the ballpark every Saturday. It was a ritual that none of us missed. Same time, same place. There was rough talk and fists and sometimes knives. It could get rough, but I was a pretty good scrapper in a fight. My small, wiry frame gave me an advantage and I was real quick. I think we were all restless and frustrated, and so far we had fought every day of our lives in one way or another. As long as I could remember I had stayed in one neighborhood, South Broad Street. But the world as I knew it was about to change.

On Dec. 7, 1941 the Japanese bombed Pearl Harbor. This was the most exciting thing that had ever happened. My brother, Bug, three years older than I, wanted to enlist in the Navy and I wanted to go, too. My mother didn't want me to go, but I kept after her to sign the papers for me, and finally she did on January 5, 1942. The next day Bug and I went to the Navy enlistment office. Bug passed all the exams and was in, but I had a little trouble. I was still a peewee and didn't weigh enough, and I also found out I was color-blind to red and green. The Navy guys told me to go across the hall and see the Army Air Force people because they needed colorblind people to see through camouflage. If it had not been for that I probably would have missed the war and my life would not be the same. In the Air Force office I still didn't weigh enough to join so they told me to go home and eat a lot of bananas, which I did. I came back the next day full of bananas and just made the weight requirement. I passed all the other tests and was now in the United States Army Air Force.

My mother eventually saw six sons leave Chattanooga to serve our country during World War II. Wesley joined the Navy, Harry went with the Sea Bees in the South Pacific, Edward was with the Army and Shang also joined the Navy. Raymond was too young then to go, but later served in the Army. Bug was sent to the Pacific War arena and it was over three years before I would see him again.

I was headed a different direction.

Off to War

B oy, I thought I was something dressed up in a uniform. I was just a kid but all of a sudden I felt like a man. I stayed nearby at Ft. Oglethorpe, Georgia for about two weeks of preliminary training, then was shipped to Barksdale Field Air Base in Shreveport, Louisiana. Boot camp was rough, it was very dusty out there and there were times I wondered why I joined, but I made it through. I took my basic training at Barksdale for about two months where I was taught to be a radio operator on a B-24D Liberator aircraft.

I was assigned to the 415th Bomb Squadron, 98th Bomb Group and then moved to Plant City, Florida, to what was to become Lakeland Air Base. We were the first servicemen to arrive so they dumped us in the middle of a palmetto field and told us to build an airfield. Which we did. I was only eighteen years old, but I had a lot of construction skills that were put to good use.

Plant City was real close to the base and we would go to the town on one-day passes. I met some wonderful people there and I was having a great time, enjoying my first experiences outside of Chattanooga. But after awhile things started to happen that woke me up.

One day a B-24 crash-landed and everyone got out except a captain. He was trapped in the plane. The plane was on fire and we could hear him screaming. It was an awful sound that I can still hear to this day. There was an officer standing in our group watching the fire and hearing the screams. He could not stand seeing the captain in the plane burning so he took out his pistol and shot the captain. Later, he was court martialed and fined a dollar, given a carton of cigarettes and one-week leave. No one blamed him, as it was impossible to get the captain out.

Another time a plane crashed in a rock pit. Everyone was killed except the tail gunner. The bodies were torn badly into pieces and I was with a group who helped retrieve the body parts. It was horrible. This is when I realized I could get killed.

My group left Florida in April of 1942 and traveled to Fort Dix in New Jersey. After more training we finally boarded a troop ship in the port of New York City on July 15, 1942. We did not know where we were going; it was all very secretive. The ship we were boarding was the Louis Pasteur – a converted French luxury liner. It was huge, about 30,000 tons and as we walked up the loading ramp I couldn't believe my eyes. What a ship. It flew a British flag and was manned by a British crew. It had big swimming pool but it was full of potatoes. There were about five thousand men on board and not enough room to bunk everyone, but I did get a tiny little bunk in the bottom of the ship.

There was no one there to see us off and we left the harbor as a single ship, not part of a convoy because this was supposed to be one of the fastest ships around. The first three days we had some air cover, but after that we were on our own. We zigzagged across the ocean, three times dodging torpedoes fired by subs. Thank God they missed. We were told if we lit a cigarette on deck at night it would be shot out of our mouths. It was pretty tense.

On board things got pretty rough because the food was terrible. We had heard that the ship had been used to transport German POW's and we believed the food was meant for them. It was rotten tasting mutton and moldy, stinky cheese. Awful, British type food. The officers were treated like royalty and given chicken and vegetables and we'd see them throw leftovers over the ship rails. I'm telling you, there was nearly a riot because of the food. To this day the thought of mutton makes me sick.

There was a special ceremony when we crossed the equator, and we stopped to refuel in Sierra Leone, Africa. We weren't allowed off ship. Finally, on August 4 we landed at Durban, South Africa and were allowed a two-day pass. It was wonderful to finally be off the ship. I went into the town to a large plaza square with a statue in the middle. There were lots of people all around the square and I met a really nice girl. I don't remember her name, but I know she later wrote to me several times.

After we set sail again the ship reached the tip of South Africa and rounded the Cape of Good Hope. We headed up between the West African coast and the island of Madagascar to the entrance of the Red Sea, then traveled the entire length of the Red Sea through the Suez Canal. After a thirty-two day, unescorted trip we landed at Port Said in Egypt. I was farther away from home than I'd ever dreamed, and in a very foreign land.

Down to Egypt

At this time we did not know why we were here in Egypt. We would find out much later. It was August of 1942 and the British ruled in this part of the world called the Middle East. We were the first group of Americans in that part of the country. After we unloaded at Port Said in Egypt we were moved to Haifa in Palestine (now Israel). There was only a landing strip there and we lived in tents. I was not assigned to any specific job then, just general duties around the base.

I made a lot of friends around the airbase. They lived in a commune called a kibbutz – Jewish young people trying to make a living on a farm in the desert. They didn't have much food, but they were willing to share it with an American friend. It was then that I learned there were a lot of people in this world that needed help. I went to the base PX and to the main cooks on our base and they would give me food to share with my new friends. I always managed to find friends anywhere I went.

After about three weeks I was offered a job as a weatherman and I jumped at the chance. It required going to weather school in Trans Jordan along with two other soldiers chosen for the job. We were stationed with the RAF, "Royal Air Force", on a British air base. The German army was under Rommel's command in the western desert, very close to Egypt. The British Army had stopped the German advance at a place called El-Alamein, near Alexandria, Egypt. If they had taken Egypt this war would have been a lot longer and a heck of a lot tougher to win. We were at this British Air Base for the sole reason of having a place for allied planes to land in the event the Germans did take Egypt.

While at this base I had some British friends and one day they asked me if I would like to go to Jerusalem with them. I got excited and said yes! When I was in school as a young boy I had studied about the Holy Land, never dreaming I would someday be there. We went by car through Jericho and I saw a wall like I had read about in the Bible. We crossed a bridge over the Jordan River where we stopped and bought some oranges. They were the first oranges I had seen since I left Florida and I do believe they were the best oranges I have ever eaten. After we left Jericho we went down to the Dead Sea, then on to Jerusalem.

We stayed in Jerusalem two days and for those two days I saw everything I could. I went down to Bethlehem to the grotto where Jesus was born. I had the strangest feeling when I went down the steps and stood in front of an alcove. There was a big star over the spot they say he was born. I have always felt blessed by being there.

When I left there I went into the old walled city of Jerusalem. The streets were very narrow. I traveled the route Jesus made when he was carrying the cross. At a spring where a woman gave him a drink of water is a stone wall where they believe he stumbled and put out his hand. So many have touched it there is now a handprint. You can clearly see it. I put my hand into it and again had a funny feeling. After my two British friends finished their business we left to go back to Tran Jordan. I was not very religious at the time, but I felt that being there had changed me in some way.

After several more months at this RAF base, we began to hear news about the war getting started again in El-Alamein. The British army started an offensive against the Germans there, breaking the German line and Rommel began to retreat. I don't think this retreat stopped until Rommel was pushed back to Tripoli, Libya. As he was pushed back our group started to move forward and we moved back down into Egypt.

Just before we moved we had an Arab who kept our tent and firing equipment clean. I think his pay from us was about a dollar day. He was a young man and we asked him why he was working. He said he was working and saving his money to get himself a bride. We couldn't understand the idea of him having to buy his bride, but that was their custom there. We asked him how long it would take him to buy his bride and he told us about ten years.

Well, we really felt sorry for him. We began to take up money from our friends and got enough to buy him his bride. You never saw as much happiness on a man's face as he had. I don't think he ever forgot us. I never saw him again after we left, but he did get his bride.

We moved again with the RAF to Benghazi, Libya and made camp on the shores of the Mediterranean Sea. We pitched our tents in a graveyard where the Germans and Italians had buried their dead after combat. Some of the tin grave markers were inside our tent. But we figured the dead couldn't hurt you, and thought that was the safest place because of the mines that had been left behind.

I learned about mines the hard way. One day a group of

us saw a German plane that had crashed and been left behind over in a field. We went over to it and were looking around when we noticed a bunch of men hollering and waving at us. We had just walked through a minefield! We sweated our way back out.

My good friend, George, an RAF soldier, and I were in a bombing raid one day. There was a big rock pit in our camp. In this rock pit there was a cave – not a large one, but this is where George and I would go for cover when the bombs were falling. Luckily none hit the rock pit. George and I used this cave for protection many times, but I have to admit we got pretty drunk in that cave, too. We had what we thought was our last cigarette more than once.

Another time the Germans were bombing us and I dove into the nearest hole I could find. There was another guy there – that made two of us in that hole. Old nosy me – I stuck my head up and just at that time a bomb went off. I got two pieces of shrapnel in my face, one just above my left eye and one just below it. Blood was everywhere, just spurting out. I managed to hold my shirt over my left eye to control the blood. After the raid was over they carried me by ambulance to Benghazi to some tents like you would see on the TV show "Mash". They got the metal out and put bandages over my face. I remember I had two holes for my eyes and one for my nose and mouth. They said the metal did not harm my eye. I carry these scars today.

We had 500-pound bombs lying everywhere and one night paratroopers dropped in on us, setting off one of the bombs lying on the ground. There were two GI's in a tent next to a chain link fence and one got up to go to the latrine while the other stayed sleeping in the tent. Before he got back, the ignited bomb blew the GI that stayed in his tent through the chain link fence. We found shredded flesh and clothing and tent all over the fence. It killed him instantly. How could it be that just getting up to go to the bathroom could save your life? I will never know the answer, but I saw many things like that.

A British plane crashed one day and caught on fire when it hit the ground. I don't know how many men were in it but I do know of one – he could not get out of the wreckage; we heard him screaming and saw him moving around. There was no way to get him out. When a plane burns it is a very hot fire. This is the second man I saw burn up in a plane crash, never realizing what was ahead for me.

Ploesti

I was promoted to sergeant and rejoined the 98th bomb group, which had moved into Benghazi, Libya, about this time. We moved out about ten miles from the city where there were runways already built by the Germans and I started drawing weather maps. Everything we did in weather was coded and we got weather reports from all over the world. It was my job to put these onto a map so the weather forecasters could predict the weather over the targets of the bombing missions. I was good at reading the different types of clouds, there are ten different types that mean different things, and I enjoyed thinking about them. I guess you could say my head was in the clouds! It is amazing how just a wobble in the atmosphere can create changes in the weather and seasons. I became more and more aware of the sky above.

At four o'clock one morning I had just stepped out of the weather trailer to get some fresh air when a ME-109 came in very low under the radar. He was firing all of his guns. There was a row of bullets on both sides of me- missed me. He destroyed a number of planes and gas tankers and got away. But he missed me.

I still have a poem that I wrote during that time in the desert. It kind of gives you and idea of what things were like out there.

Somewhere in the Middle East
>Somewhere in the Middle East where the sun
>is hot and dry,
>Where a hundred fresh mosquitoes replace
>each one that die,
>Where all the men wish and dream of a fair
>and greener land,
>And wake up in the morning with their hands
>full of sand.
>
>Somewhere in the Middle East where a girl is
>never seen,
>Where the sky is never cloudy and the grass is
>never green,
>Where the moon is like a searchlight and the
>night is made for love,
>Where the stars keep shining like a northern
>cross above.
>
>Somewhere in the Middle East where green
>grass never grows,
>Where camels take the place of trains and a
>rooster never crows,

Where desert winds and pestering flies are
busy on retreat,
And taking back a foul smell of Rommel's
stinky feet.

Somewhere in the Middle East where the beer
is weak and stale,
Where coffee tastes like tobacco juice-like the
kind you'd get in jail,
Where the days are hot and nights are cold
and the desert wind will say,
"Take me back to Philly in the good old
U.S.A."

The times I enjoyed most then were when I would get a
three-day pass to Cairo, Egypt. I would catch a ride on a
bomber that was going that way and catch a ride back. I saw
the Sphinx and went inside and around the Pyramids. I could
not believe my eyes. I had come a long way from South Broad
Street.

Sometimes I would go to Tel Aviv, Palestine to see my Jewish friends. Some of them were in the Army and some civilians, but they made me feel like I was a part of them, like I was family. We would go to the beach or to their homes for dinner. I was nineteen and had become a citizen of the world.

Our planes had been on a lot of low altitude training flights for some reason, altitudes between 50 and 300 feet. This went on for weeks until we finally found out what the secrecy was all about, the mission that brought our group to Egypt in the beginning.

It was the low-level attack on the Ploesti Oil fields in Romania. Ploesti was the major source of oil and gas for the German army and this low-level surprise attack was supposed to destroy the oil fields and refineries. The only problem was that Ploesti was Germany's most heavily defended target. The plan was to go in low, under radar, and surprise the enemy.

The flight commander of the 98th bomb group was Colonel John "Killer" Kane, and our target was two oil refinery and storage complexes in Romania, over a thousand miles away. This meant a seven-hour flight over there, all at low altitudes. We were one of several bomb groups on the mission and we were called the Pyramiders because of our training in Egypt. Our planes were painted a desert pink.

We were briefed that fifty percent of our planes might not come back, but that if the mission was accomplished we could end the war in six months. That sounded like a good thing so we all got ready. As a weatherman I did not fly on missions, but I still felt the tension and the importance of this mission. It was real quiet the night before the mission. Most of the crew wrote letters to their family. The letter could not be mailed until the mission was over.

Early Sunday morning, August 1, 1943, we got word that extra men were needed to replace some crewmembers that were sick. They could not send a plane into battle with a short crew. I volunteered to go and soon found myself in one of 177 bombers lined up for take off. I took the place of a left waist gunner.

From the beginning things did not go well. One of the lead B-24 Bombers in our squad came down the runway but it could not leave the ground. It crashed and men died instantly. As far as I know all the rest of the planes made it off. Many of them did not make it back.

Anything that could go wrong went wrong that day. Somewhere over Greece we hit clouds with zero visibility, which broke up the formation and separated the groups of bombers. Radio contact was broken when some of the planes made a wrong turn and ended up over Bucharest, the German air command headquarters, letting the Germans know we were there.

All I know for sure is that they were waiting for us. Our planes were so low I could see the Germans running on the ground. We were at the treetops. The gunners were shooting at the Germans and their barracks, oil tanks, anything else they could. Huge, thousand foot billows of black smoke were everywhere and some delayed action bombs went off just as bombers were flying over them. I saw some of the planes crash into the oil tanks, some blew up. I've heard it called the most hellish mission of the entire war and for good reason. It was a fiery hell on earth.

We lost 54 bombers on this mission, 54 out of 177. Hundreds of American fliers lost their lives in one day, almost a third of our men. I was now twenty years old and I lost a lot of my friends on this mission. The American people need to know about Ploesti and the lives that were given that day. Colonel Kane and four others received Congressional Medals of Honor, the most given for any one mission of the war.

We did some damage but not enough to stop the refineries from fueling Hitler's war machine. Our B-24 made it back but it was full of huge holes. I don't believe a one got back that wasn't damaged- the hole wasn't only in the fuselage, but in the wings, tail, you name it. There was one that was almost torn in half. But it made it back. We did not destroy the oil fields like it was planned, but we knew it was one of the most important targets that could end the war. Ploesti continued to be a target and I would see it again.

The Eleventh Man

My bomber group stayed in Benghazi for several months before we moved up the coast of the Mediterranean Sea. Italy had surrendered by this time and we then moved to an airbase in Lecce, near Brindisi, Italy. I remember meeting and falling in love with a wonderful Italian girl. I don't remember her name. Her father got very upset when he realized how we felt about each other. He sent her away and I can still see her in the window of the train waving at me as it left the station.

I was still doing weather maps at this time, but I got to thinking- if I started flying, I could get fifty missions in and go home. That was the rule then. Originally we had been told that you could go home after flying twenty-five missions, but by now the number had increased to fifty. There was an opening in the group for a cameraman, so I put in and got the job. I made staff sergeant at this time and a new position as cameraman. I was now going to go on bombing missions.

There was a ten-man crew on a B-24 who flew the same plane for every mission and became a very tight unit. The cameraman was always the eleventh man and usually flew in the last bomber in the formation in order to get pictures of the damage done by the mission. The only problem was that the enemy was fully engaged by that time, making it the most vulnerable flight position. To be in that last plane every time increased the odds of getting shot down and not making it home at all, in fact very few cameramen did. The chances of a cameraman making fifty missions were pretty much zero. But I did not know any of this. I saw it as a way to get home.

And so I became the eleventh man, flying with a different crew on just about every mission. I was the cameraman. I had a K17 camera mounted in the escape hatch in the floor in the back of the plane. This escape hatch would have been used to bail out on other planes without a camera. The camera filled up the whole hatch in the floor. It was about two-by-three feet wide and about four feet tall, extending beneath the plane. I could move it in almost any direction. The only other openings in the back of the plane were the left and right windows, which had a .50 caliber gun in each window.

On a B-24 there were six gunner positions, all with .50 caliber machine guns in place. In the front there was a nose gun and top turret gun, and in the back there was the tail gun, ball turret gun (in the floor) and right and left waist guns. This made a lot of fire power, but it didn't stop the flak or the enemy planes- they had twenty millimeter canons and rockets on theirs. One of the advantages of having an eleventh man on board was that if any one of the gunners was wounded or killed, I would take his place as a gunner. I was excited to be getting up into the air and seeing some action. I bought a white scarf to wear with my bomber jacket and thought I was something. Plus it was going to be cold up there.

So far the combat activity I had seen had been random or on the ground. Now I was entering daily contact with the enemy and never knew where I might be headed. I flew over Ploesti five more times as we kept hammering the German oil supply. There were missions in the Balkans; some were over Austria or anywhere within the range of our bombers. There never was a mission that we didn't lose several planes. One day I saw ten bombers go down in fifteen minutes and very few parachutes.

The anti-air craft fire over the target is something you could hardly believe. The black smoke from the anti-aircraft was so thick you thought you could get out and walk on it. The flak was everywhere, yards and yards of exploding shrapnel coming at you. Then after you left the target the German fighter planes would take over. There were many times our bomber would be hit by anti-aircraft fire and German fighters, the crew would be wounded, but we'd manage to make it back.

On one of our missions to Austria we were hit real bad. Most of the tail on our plane was shot away. It knocked us out of formation- that was usually the end of you. But this time we came back on the west side of Italy, the side that Naples was on. It was March of 1944 and Mt. Vesuvius was erupting- we could see lava running down the side of the mountain like bright orange ribbons. I'll never forget that sight.

We got back to our base about two hours after the rest of the group did. They had given us up for lost and had taken all of our personal things to the supply depot for shipment home. We fooled them this time. They had to bring our personal things back. I was still alive, mission after mission, trying to get home.

The 29ᵗʰ Mission

Before dawn on the morning of May 29, 1944, I was at the landing strip getting ready to fly with the crew of *Hell's Belles*, a B24J. We were waiting on the rest of the crew – pilot, co-pilot, bombers and navigator, who were at the officer's briefing. The rest of us were at the plane getting it ready to go. We never knew what or where the mission would be until we got airborne. The target that day was a ball bearings factory in Wiener – Neustadt, Austria. I had been over this target before with other crews. It was deep in enemy land and well fortified with anti-aircraft guns and fighter planes. We had lost a lot of planes over this target in the past. Knowing this did not make me feel any better.

This was my twenty-ninth mission. I needed twenty-one more before they would send me home. I did not know any of the crew at the time we left our base. This crew was on their fifth mission and we were flying at the tail end of our formation. We were doing quite well over the Adriatic Sea until we hit the coastline of Northern Italy. The anti-aircraft fire was bad and it was staying with us all the way to the target.

The night before, the land crew had changed an engine on the right side of our plane. We didn't know it at the time but apparently they didn't have time to check it out. We were about twenty miles from the target when the oil pressure dropped in that engine. This engine was on the outside of the right wing. We couldn't keep up with the rest of the group. Our bombers dropped the bombs we were carrying to try to keep up. We still could not on three engines. You could fly a B-24 on three engines but you couldn't keep up. We were told to wait and try and get in a formation of B-24's on the way back from the target. We waited but somehow we could not find any B-24's. The crew in the back did not know too much about what was going on. I think our pilot might have thought we could try and make it back on our own. When a plane drops out of formation it becomes a sitting duck for the fighters. That is exactly what happened.

The fighter planes swarmed over us like a bunch of flies. You could see bullets flying all over the place. All of our guns were firing. All I could do at the moment was stand there and watch the left and right waist gunners. The right waist gunner went down. I grabbed his gun and started firing. I glanced around and saw that his right foot at the ankle was shot away. I didn't see any blood, just white bone where his ankle had been. He looked at me so pitiful; I never will forget his face. There was nothing I could do at the moment. The safety of the plane was more important than anything. We were all firing at the German fighters; they were coming at all angles. I heard the tail gunner quit firing, no sound from his turret. At this time I felt a blow on the bottom of my left foot that felt like a sledgehammer hit it. I later found out that half of my heel was shot away – on my boot, not my foot. All of this time I didn't have time to be scared. That would come later.

The second engine was shot out on the same side. That put us in a real bad situation. I heard someone on the intercom say, "B-24 coming on our tail." I looked and saw they were ME-110 fighters. They had twin tails like a B-24 and they also had rocket guns under their wings, which at first glance you would have thought they were B-24's. I remember saying over the phone, "B-24-hell, they are ME-110's!"

Then the left gunner went down. You could hear and see the bullets hitting our plane and about this time they shot out the third engine. There was no doubt we were going down. I think at this time we were at about fifteen thousand feet. We began to lose altitude fast and starting circling down. I looked down at the parachute on the front of my chest. All this time I had been in the war, I had never had any training on how to open a parachute.

It was about this time my flight engineer, Don Kennedy, was coming across the cat walk to help the right gunner that was down. There was just me and the ball turret gunner left in the back still firing. When Don got to the end of the catwalk, the ball turret gunner stood up out of his turret just as a rocket was coming from the left side of the plane. I was standing by my gun with high-octane gas flying over me like a shower. The rocket hit the ball turret gunner and blew him all to pieces. If it had not hit the ball turret gunner it would have hit me. I was in the direct line of it, but he stood up in front of me right at that very moment.

I remember a big wall of fire and the next thing I remember was spinning in the air. I did not jump. I was blown through the side of the plane under the right waist gun window. I threw out my arms to straighten myself up. I pulled the ripcord on my chest. This was when I got real scared. The chute did not open. The only thing I could figure out was the ripcord was cut. I began tearing at the chute with my hands and it finally opened.

The good Lord was with me that day. As I was coming down in my chute there was an ME-109 coming straight at me. My first thought was he was going to shoot me with his machine guns. I had seen this happen before when some of our airmen came down. He slowed his plane down real slow – he was about a hundred feet from me. I went limp in my chute. I thought this was it. Instead, he wobbled his wings and waved at me. I waved back. We looked right at each other. I'll never know who this man was, but I hope he made it through the war. Because he had a heart.

I was still a ways from the ground. After hearing all of the shells and rockets and the roar of plane engines it became very quiet. I could hear the birds singing. I felt something warm running down my leg. I thought it was blood but turned out it was my own urine. There were small pieces of metal in my face and arms, I guess from the rocket that hit my ball turret gunner. Small pieces of his flesh were all over me. I had to wear those clothes several weeks before I could get some more.

When I was close to the ground I could see a house below me. I was landing in the Alps, and there was just one house in a large area of trees. I landed in the yard of that house and hit so hard I went backwards. It must have knocked me out for a few seconds. When I came to I rolled my chute in a ball. There was a well just a few feet from where I landed and I threw my chute into it. We had heard that the women in these countries would get our chutes and make under clothes out of them since they were made out of nylon. I could not see anyone at that moment.

I didn't know it at the time but someone was in the house.

I guess they were about as scared as I was. I stopped for a minute and knelt down on the ground and thanked the Good Lord that I was alive. I was starting across the yard to get to some woods close by, when a little girl about ten years old came across the yard and took me by the hand. She was a little blonde-haired girl and she did not say a word. She pulled me by the hand as if to say, "Come with me." She led me into the house where there were two young women. They also did not say a word. They wanted me to follow them. I guess they thought I was hurt real bad. They carried me into a room where there was a bed and had me lie down on it. I knew there was an underground group in Austria and I thought maybe I had found it.

A short time later, a group of civilians came into the room and they talked amongst themselves for a few minutes. Then one man motioned for me to get up and follow him. I was limping on my right leg, which I found out years later was broken above my right knee. I had a limp for quite awhile after that.

There were about twenty-five men altogether and they all had guns. I was doing pretty good until I saw something sitting in the yard. It was a wheel cart hooked to a mule carrying an old fashioned wooden coffin. It was empty with no lid. About that time I really started talking to the good Lord.

They put me behind the cart and we started walking. Could you believe how I felt- twenty-five men with guns surrounding me. Every once in a while I could see a barrel pointed at me, I don't know if it was on purpose or not. But the barrel seemed to be about four inches wide.

We were on an old trail that was really rough, and we walked about an hour before stopping to rest in a clearing. I was sitting alone and the others were all around me. None of them spoke English. There was a little dog with them and he came over to me. I have always thought that little dog knew I needed a friend. I started petting him, when an older man called the dog back to him. He pointed to me and pointed up to the clearing and patted his rifle. There was no doubt in my mind what he meant. This was the day and the minute I really started believing in God. May 29, 1944.

I started praying and just sitting there, it wasn't long before the men got up and we started again. I was still walking behind the empty coffin. I needed some water real bad, but they didn't give me any. It wasn't long before we stopped again and they motioned for me to sit down again. They then moved the empty coffin into some woods.

About 45 minutes later they came out of the woods again. They brought the coffin on the cart and stopped in front of me. They still didn't say anything. The coffin was not empty now; there was a body in it. They wanted me to look at it and I did. It was the body of my right waist gunner, the one that had his foot blown off at the ankle. I could not understand what they were saying, but by gesture and motions I finally understood. Somehow, he had gotten out of the plane and opened his chute, had landed in a tree and his chute was tangled in the branches. He must have bled to death. The coffin was not for me, but for Z. V. Penny, my right waist gunner.

They put me behind the cart again and we started walking. The trail was very rough and the cart would bounce the body around. Every so often I would have to put him back in the coffin. It was terrible.

After about one hour we came to an alpine village that looked something you'd see on a postcard. There was a low wall in front of this big chateau and they sat me down on it. I think everyone in the village came to see me, young and old. I was so thirsty. By this time I finally asked for a drink of water and in a few minutes I had a jug of water. I think the name of this village was Fishbau, Austria.

They carried the cart and coffin away and I was put in a barn with a window with bars on it. The room was about twenty feet by six feet, like a hallway with one door and one window. Inside were two sawhorses with some boards on it. This was supposed to be my bed. I think the whole village crowded around the door. There was one man who spoke English and he asked me when I had eaten last. I told him about three o'clock that morning, about twelve hours earlier. He said something to the crowd and they vanished. About twenty minutes later they were back with arms full of food and water, pillows, and all kinds of soft, warm blankets to cover the boards. I could not believe this after all I had been through that day.

It all lasted a few minutes, then he sent them away. We were now alone. They had found the plane, he said, and wanted to know if the round things in it were bombs. There were bodies in the plane and they wanted to get them out and bury them. He then said something to me that I'll never forget. He said, "When you get back to America, tell the American people how the Austrians have treated you."

I'm finally keeping my promise. They treated me like I was a king.

He then left and I was looking through the bars of the window and saw them bury my right waist gunner. I realized the strangest thing- from the moment I hit the ground till I was left alone in my cell, they never did search me for weapons.

I ate some of the food they brought me, and by this time I was very tired. I made a bed on the sawhorses and boards out of the blankets they had brought me. It was dark when I lay down. The day's events caught up with me. I was thinking what the future was going to be for me. I started reliving the events that had happened that day in my mind. I remembered that when I was blown out of the plane and got my chute open, I only saw two more chutes besides my own. That's all I saw out of eleven men on board. My right waist gunner and I was all I could account for. I wondered what had happened to the other nine men. Then, I think I passed out.

Captivity

About four o'clock the next morning a soldier came to my cell and took me to a building close by. There was another soldier sitting behind a desk. He spoke English and told me to empty my pockets on the desk. I did what he told me to do. He went through my billfold and took everything out of it, dollars, identification cards, and other things I had in it. He kept my watch, ring, escape packet and the things in my billfold. He also took my flight jacket and my white scarf. At this time I did not think about the underground anymore. I may have found what had been the underground, but they had been taken over. This man was a German soldier.

The soldier that brought me to him tapped me on the shoulder and motioned for me to follow him outside. It was still dark, and he took me to a house close by and sat me down at the kitchen table. In a few minutes two girls came into the kitchen and started cooking eggs and bacon. We all four ate breakfast together and I must say the girls were very pretty. They spoke broken English. I didn't know it then, but these two girls would be the last females I would get to talk to for a long time.

After we had breakfast and coffee (I think the coffee was made out of burnt acorns) we got up and went out of the building onto a path. We were still up in the Austrian Mountains. The soldier had a rifle and he and the two girls went in front of me, all three of them laughing and cutting up. I remembered that in four days I would be twenty-one years old.

As we went down the mountain, I did not know where

we were going. The soldier and the two girls were about one block in front of me and I could have escaped. But where would I go? After about two hours of walking we came to a small town where there was a railroad station. There I was reunited with the men from my crew that had survived and found out what happened to everyone else.

Tail gunner, left waist gunner, right waist gunner, ball turret gunner, all four in the back died except me. I was the only one in the back of the plane that was alive, the eleventh man. In front the nose turret gunner could not get out of his turret because the hydraulics had frozen. There is only one way in and one way out of a turret. If it is not lined up just right you cannot get out. His turret was not, and he went down with the plane. There were eleven men on board and five were killed. Surviving were three officers and three enlisted men, including me. As I said before I saw only two chutes besides my own. One was the right waist gunner who died in the tree, Z. V. Penny, and the other was Don Kennedy, flight engineer. Don Kennedy had also never flown with this crew because he had replaced a sick crewmember at the last minute. We really didn't know any of them.

We were all put together in a small room on a train where we could talk and try to find out what happened. Don and Ed Follet, radio operator, were burned about their faces real bad from the fire on the plane and were bandaged from their shoulders to the top of their heads. All you could see was two holes for their eyes, one for their nose and one for their mouth. The only way I could tell who they were was that Don was a small man and Ed was a big man. Don wanted a cigarette and we lit one and stuck it in the hole for his mouth because his hands were bandaged also. You should have seen the smoke coming out of Don's bandages. My pants were burned pretty badly. From the knee down one leg was gone and the other was in rags. They would put other people in our room. As long as they were in there we did not say a word. You never know.

The train carried us first to Vienna, Austria, then to Frankfurt Germany. Frankfurt was an Interrogation Center. There they separated us and put us in different cells. There was a man in my cell when they put me in there and he spoke perfect English. That's what gave him away. He asked me all kinds of questions. I told him he should not be talking like this as I had no doubt this cell was bugged (and I suspected he was German). In about ten minutes they came and got him and I was left alone. I never did answer any of his questions.

I don't know how long I stayed in that cell but it was hours. Finally a guard came and got me and took me to an office. There was a German officer sitting at a desk. I sat in a chair at the end of the desk. He started asking me questions. I would answer name, rank and serial number. He then pulled out a file about half inch thick. He started telling me where I was born and lived, where I went to school, name of my outfit, my parents' name and things like that. I just sat there dumbfounded. He then dropped a bombshell. He said, "You were a cameraman on this plane, and I guess you know we shoot all cameramen as spies." I believed he meant it.

Name, rank and serial number, was all I said. The guard came and took me to another cell. I believe the date was May 30, 1944. In three more days I would be twenty-one years old. Happy Birthday! I hope nobody ever has to celebrate their birthday like this one.

The other prisoners of war and I were put in boxcars like cattle, standing room only, no windows or air. The train rattled with us down the track until we stopped in a railroad yard and the guards told us, "This is Berlin." We didn't know why we were stopped. We soon found out. We were in an allied air raid and no trains were allowed to move during an air raid. They kept us there in the rail yard, standing in the boxcars for two days and three nights with bombs dropping all around us. Our boxcar would shake when a bomb hit close by. They would not let us out. Standing room only, we went to the bathroom in our clothes. I think we were all sick from the smell. This is where I finally had my birthday. I always said I would celebrate my twenty-first birthday with a bang. I think I did, don't you?

Finally, the raid ended, the train started again and we got out of Berlin. They gave us some food and water. We needed water worse than anything and were hoping the trip wouldn't last too much longer. The train stopped again and we thought we had reached our destination, but were we ever wrong. This time the tracks in front of us had been blown up by the raids and the train couldn't pass, so we were taken out of the boxcars and loaded into trucks. I lost contact with the rest of the crew because they were put on different trucks. The truck I was in carried us about eighty miles to a camp outside of Weimer, Germany. Its name was Buchenwald.

I am not going to say very much about the next three weeks I spent in this camp because I have seen so much footage over the years of what was going on there at the time, and it gets mixed in with my memories. I want to be as accurate as I can about everything I saw. I mainly want it to be known that I was there. I saw it with my own eyes.

It was clear from the start that a mistake had been made. The German officers at the camp made a big stink when we arrived. This was not the right camp and we were not supposed to be there. We were put in some wooden barracks that were separated from the rest of the camp by a barbed wire fence. I could see men in striped dirty rags that looked like walking skeletons. They were all sunken in and you could tell they were starving. I saw bodies stacked up like cords of wood. I saw thousands of men, woman and children coming in each day on the trains. I heard the guards yelling at them, "Juden, Juden."

We had Jewish flyers with us and we were afraid they would be taken away. I thought of my Jewish friends I had left behind in Palestine, of the happy times we had together at the beach. I hoped they were safe. We knew it was a death camp for the Jewish people without anyone telling us anything. It was real, it happened, I saw it. Don't ever let anybody tell you it didn't.

I guess the tracks got fixed because one day they crammed us back up into boxcars. We finally came into a train station in Northern Poland near the Baltic Sea, Kiefheide station, near Gross Tychow. They let us out of the boxcars and we walked about 3 miles to the camp; Stalag Luft IV was the name of it. After the war it was known for being one of the worst.

We walked through a forest of trees into a clearing where the camp had been built. It was divided into four compounds, A-B-C-D, and we walked through the gate into compound A. I saw machine gun towers with huge spotlights all around the camp. It was surrounded by two ten-foot high barbed wire fences about twenty feet apart. There was a four-foot high roll of razor wire in between the fences. About thirty feet inside the fence there was a two-by-four rail about three feet tall. This was no-man's land, and if you crossed that rail you would be shot.

I've always wondered if whoever made the show *Hogan's Heroes* had been there, because the camp looked very much like that. Each of the four compounds had ten wooden barracks, three feet off the ground. They were about eighty feet long. There was a long hall in the middle of the barrack with rooms on each side of it. The rooms were about eighteen feet square with one window and one door. The bunks were made of wood, three layers high with a thin mattress of hay. There were wooden slats on the bottom of the bed about twelve inches apart. No pillow. There was a small stove, a small table, and some benches in the room. The window had wooden shutters on it and we were locked in at night. There were twenty-six men in one room built to house fifteen. There was no ventilation in the room. Can you imagine the humidity in there? Plus all the snoring!

There was one latrine per barrack, a makeshift board with two holes in it. There was one small shower building in each compound. No hot water, winter or summer, and there was enough space for about four men to shower at once.

All the food we ate was boiled, what there was of it. We had boiled potatoes twice a day. Sometimes they would bring in a dead horse for meat. It would be cut up and put in with the potatoes. Every morning a man from each room was sent with a two-gallon bucket to the kitchen. They would fill it up with potatoes. They would bring it back to each room and we would peel the potatoes and send them back to the kitchen. A lot of times I would keep the peelings off the potatoes and cook them on our little stove. There never was any left. We ate them all.

There were twenty-five hundred men in compound A and twice a day, seven days a week, we would have roll call, rain or shine or snow. We would take turns staying in the barracks pretending we were asleep or something to that effect. We did this to mess up the roll call and count. We did all kinds of things to mess it up. The bad part of it was we would have to stand in formation till the count was correct. The Germans finally caught on to us doing this.

At night the searchlights stayed on all night. The guards walked around the compound at night with German Shepherds and sometimes they would turn them loose. You did not go out at night. I remember one night the kitchen was short of men for some reason and they sent word to our barracks to send help. I was one of the men sent to the kitchen. There were six of us men crossing the compound at night. No guards were with us. That was a strange feeling crossing the compound with all the searchlights roaming around. I felt a lot better when we got inside. We stayed all night.

We were supposed to receive a Red Cross parcel once a week. To start out they gave us one a month per man. Later they changed it to one a month for six men. The Red Cross parcels contained powdered milk, which was called KILM. Milk spelled backwards. There were cigarettes, canned meat, cookies and food with a high protein content. If it were not for the Red Cross parcels I believe a lot of us would have starved to death.

Food was the main thing we talked about. You'd think a bunch of men locked up with no women would talk about sex. Wrong. You think about food, then sex. We'd talk about how big the steak was we were going to eat when we got out of there. Somehow that steak kept growing until it was about three-foot across and six inches deep.

We did not have to work like the Russians and Polish POWs. Their camp was on the outside of compound A. One day I was walking around by the guardrail, no-mans-land, when something hit my foot. I looked down and saw a metal object. A Russian POW was on the other side of the fence and he threw up his hand like he was waving at me. I knew what is was then – it was a part we needed for our underground radio. I picked it up and walked into a group of men playing ball, to keep from being noticed by the guards. I turned it over to the man who had the radio. They were very glad to get it; we could then get outside news about the war.

Getting news from the outside gave our morale a great boost. News would be heard and carried from one bunk to another. That's how we did it. The little table in our room had a smooth place on the bottom. I drew a map on it so we could know where the fronts were so we could keep up with the war.

One of the German guards was so big, about 6'6", 200 pounds, that he had to stoop to get through the door. We called him Big Stoop. His hands were twice the size of mine and he was known for hitting prisoners on the ears with them, sometimes bursting their eardrums. He was one of the meanest and most hated guards we had.

One day Big Stoop came into our room and went straight to the table. He turned it over and saw my map. He turned straight to me and started beating me. The other men in the room could not do a thing about it. I thought he was going to kill me. I was down on the floor when I saw him go to the table and smash it to pieces. Somebody had to have told him about my map. We had very little medical care, but I got through this OK.

Life in a POW camp meant you had to be very careful

about everything you did. There were a lot of rules and you could be shot if you broke them. One day we heard a lot of shouting and we saw one of our buddies step across the dead rail into no-man's-land. We were calling to him to come back, even the guards in the machine guard tower were hollering for him to go back. He turned to us and said very calmly, "I'm going to see my mother." He got to the fence and the guards in the tower cut him to pieces with their machine guns.

Another time one of my buddies hopped out of a window instead of going out the door. There was a guard outside the fence on the ground. He shot this man with his rifle – the bullet went through his heart. It killed him instantly. Where he laid on the ground his blood made a perfect V. I wish I could have had a camera to get a picture of this shooting for no reason at all. He shot my buddy just for jumping out the window. The rules said: out the door, no windows. His name was Aubrey Teague.

In our Red Cross parcel we got a little sewing kit. It was made out of cloth and was red and blue. We used those kits to make little American flags. I know of at least thirteen men who were killed in the camps and we used these flags to put on the blanket of each man who was buried. As far as I know there never was a man buried without a flag and I helped make the one for Aubrey Teague's blanket.

Another time there was a German guard climbing up a light pole in the center of the four compounds. I guess he was fixing something. The line he was working on was a high power line and he came in contact with one of the lines and it cooked him. You could see and smell him burning. Here was something we should not have done, but we did. He was the enemy. We started cheering and yelling and waving our arms. Just about this time I believe all the machine guns in the towers cut loose. Bullets were flying everywhere-men running all over the place. I ran down the hall of our barracks to the latrine. It was made of concrete so I ran through the door and hit the floor rolling. In just a few minutes that room was packed with men on top of each other. We could not believe it when it was over. No one was hit, but it scared the hell out of us. Most of the guards there were old men and young kids. Some of them, especially the young ones, hated the American fliers because of all the damage we did to Germany.

Life in the camp was also pretty boring. We played cards, using cigarettes for money. Most of the time we would just walk around the dead line to get exercise. I counted all the fence posts on both fences. I started to count the barbs on the barbed wire. Then things started to heat up.

See photos of Stalag Luft IV at www.B24.net

Death March

We were told that we had to evacuate the camp and we had three days to get ready. They did not tell us why but we knew – the Russian army was advancing and was about to overrun us. The Germans did not want ten thousand airmen set free to fly again. They told us we were only going to go three miles to the train station. We thought by taking the train we would be taken to another POW camp. Boy, did we get fooled.

It was February 6, 1945, when about twenty-five hundred of us walked through the gates of compound A, in a column of four men abreast. We left the camp just about 6:00 a.m. and it was real cold. Winter in Poland is very cold, and this was one of the coldest ever recorded. There was snow on the ground, about fourteen inches. We had on our overcoats, pants, shirt, sweatshirt and shoes, socks – that's about it.

As we went out of the compound they marched us by the warehouse. To our surprise, after getting one Red Cross box for six men a month, that warehouse was stacked to the ceiling with Red Cross boxes. As we went by they gave each man a box. It weighed about thirty pounds. We were stuffing the contents of the boxes in our pants, coat, anywhere we could stick something! It wasn't too bad at first. Then they started running us. We didn't know why, but no matter – when you're getting stuck with bayonets and police dogs nipping at your butt, you run. It did not take long to see that we could not keep up this pace and carry our Red Cross boxes in our pockets. We started to throw some of the stuff we least needed

by the side of the road. We could see the guards coming behind us picking up the stuff. We finally slowed down to a
walk. I don't think the guards could keep up with us running.

We walked all day without stopping. We thought we
would soon get to the train station, but they never intended to
take us to the station. We walked about ten miles that first
day. We came to a field just before dark that was covered
with about a foot of snow. The guards told us to bed down.
Each man had one blanket. What were we supposed to sleep
on? There were pine trees all around this field so a group of
us started breaking branches off them and piled them up in a
big pile. We put two blankets on top of the pile and two blankets on top of us, making room for four to sleep. All of the
other men did the same thing. We had no way of building a
fire and we did not get food that night or the next morning.

It snowed that night about ten more inches and covered
us up like little mounds. It also dropped down to about zero
degrees and froze the snow over us. Before daybreak they
got us up. You could hear popping sounds all over the place
from the ice breaking as we came out of our makeshift sleeping quarters. They started marching us again. We had no idea
where we were going and this went on day after day.

Ed Follett and myself and two other men got together.
We called one of the men Tex because he was from Texas.
They called me Chat because I was from Chattanooga, Ten-
nessee. Ed, Tex and I stayed together all through this march.
We called ourselves a combine – and all the other men of the
group did the same. We did this so we could look after each
other. Out of all the men in the camp, Ed and I were together
again. He had been the radio operator on the crew of *Hell's
Belles*. We had been shot down together and now we were on
this march together. We didn't talk about it and I don't think
Ed knew that I had been on the plane since I wasn't a regular

member of the crew.

We entered Germany at a town called Swinemunde on the Baltic. By now we had been separated into smaller groups and this field we were sleeping in had been used by a group before us. There were human feces all over the place. There was no latrine; you had to go where you could. There was no way to wash your hands or anything else. Good water was scarce on this march. The water was bad; no fresh water could be had. Most of our water came out of the ditch along the side of the road we were on. Can you think how many men urinated in the ditches?

Dysentery killed a lot of men. I had it along with Ed and Tex. You could smell us a mile away. The men got so weak from diarrhea, they could hardly walk. They had one horse and wagon that would hold about eight men when they could not walk anymore. Sometimes you would see a guard and one of our men go into the woods and hear a shot. The guard would come back by himself. Between diarrhea, pneumonia, and the trips to the woods we lost a lot of men.

I don't know which was worse, the cold or the hunger. We made little blowers with cranks on them out of some tin cans. They really did work; we could boil water in about three minutes. We would steal anything for food we could get our hands on. We would collect acorns, parch them in a fire and grind them up to make coffee out of them. We would get the roots off of grasses and cook them in our little tin cookers. We would catch grasshoppers or anything we thought was edible. You will eat anything when you were as hungry as we were. Sometimes we would get boiled potatoes if we were at a farmhouse.

They would not let us stop when we were marching if we saw a dead animal of any sort. The column would swing over to the side of the road and cut off a chunk of whatever it was. Dead horses, dogs, rabbits, you name it. Some were killed by bombing and strafing or just died. We would cook the meat later and share it among ourselves.

One time we were coming to a small town and we asked a German guard about some fresh water. He said sure, water was the cheapest thing Germany had. When we got into the village there were two-gallon buckets along side the road. As we got near to them the people of the village would kick them over and laugh. We didn't try this anymore.

To make matters worse, we got body lice in our clothes; they were as big as flies. You could lay your sweatshirt on the ground at night and it would move by itself. We would pick them off, but it did not do any good. Eggs hatched and we had them all over again. There was no way to take a bath or wash in any way. It was so cold and I think it snowed every day in February and March, some in April. We trudged along, day after day, putting one foot in front of the other. I cannot tell you how miserable it was.

They walked us in circles. They really had no place for us to go. We kept walking deeper into Germany; the 2500 men from compound A kept being broken into smaller groups. Sometimes we would sleep in open fields, sometimes in the barns on some farms. I remember one time we stopped at a barn for the night and there were big bags of barley in it. We tied strings around our pants legs and filled our pant legs full of barley. We ate it raw as we walked. You should see grown men walking stiff legged with the barley in their pants.

The Germans had tents, we didn't. We had come to a farm and the captain called twenty-five men up to his tent and I was one of them. I told Ed and Tex that if I could get on the cook detail we could eat. I was wrong; it was not a cook detail. The captain took all the men's names and said that if anything on this farm were disturbed he would hang every one of us. I believe he would have, too. We stayed up all night to keep anything from happening. It didn't. We were still alive.

One day as were walking a British fighter plane strafed our column. I don't know how many men he killed – he must have thought we were German soldiers. Another time an American plane did the same thing. All we could do was hit the ditches and run into the fields. Now you can see why we called it the Death March!

I got real sick with dysentery and in a couple of days I could not walk anymore. I passed out and I don't remember anything else. Ed said I was out of this world. That's the words he used when he told me what happened. Ed was a big man and I might have weighed about a hundred pounds by now. He *carried* me for three days. He did not say how he did this, over his shoulders or head. Ed saved my life and I never will forget him. He was a hero if there ever was one. Nobody but me knows what he did, but he saved my life. That was the only way any of us survived on this death march: we took care of each other. I mean it; we really took care of each other. It somehow made it bearable.

We were still in Germany and we went through a city named Stettin. There was a large bridge we had to cross and it had what looked like 500-lb. bombs planted all along each side of the road. What would you have thought if you had been me at the time? All I could think by then was I hope and pray they don't set these bombs off now.

Because we had been broken down into groups some walked only about 250-300 miles, some about 550-600 miles. The group Ed and I were in walked 800 miles in 86 days. Dr. Caplan, an American doctor who also was with us as a POW testified at the Nuremberg Trials after the war. He told the court just how bad the death march was; it is on the record.

The only day in those 86 that we did not march was the day President Roosevelt died. April 12, 1945. For some reason they did not make us march. At this time we really needed the rest, those that was still alive and still could walk. I was one of them.

The weather got warmer as walked deeper into Germany, and farther into April. The snow had stopped, thank the Lord. I never in my life saw snowflakes as big as those that were in Germany and Poland that winter of 1945.

Liberation

L ate in April 1945, we could hear big guns firing in the distance. We did not know if it was the Russians, Americans, or British. As it crept into May, they got louder. We knew we were close to the front lines, wherever they were.

We noticed the German guards were acting funny, kind of nervous. One day they put us in a barn on a farm. Late that afternoon, just before dark, I saw an open window in a small shed. We had not had any food in three days except what we could find or steal. There was a guard about fifteen feet away from this shed. At this time I was so hungry I didn't care, so I crawled to the window hoping the guard didn't see me. I looked in and saw some wooden barrels in there. I believed they had some food of some sort in them, so I eased through the window. I looked in the barrels and found salt pork. I grabbed as much as I could and put it through the window to Ed. As I crawled back through the window I saw the guard standing there where he had been before and he still didn't say anything. I believe to this day that he saw me. We got the salt pork and some of the others had found some potatoes. I think we really needed that salt as we did not have any on the march. We had enough food for about twenty men. Some of them got sick after no food for three days.

As we tried to find places to sleep that night we could hear the guns quite loudly. We still had no idea about what was about to happen. When we awoke the next morning, May 2, 1945, we noticed some of the guards were missing. There were a few left but they didn't say anything. Later that morning we realized what was happening. We heard the rumble of heavy equipment. About 10:00 a.m. that morning a convoy of British tanks came down the road. The British soldiers on the tanks started throwing us candy bars, food and cigarettes. We then knew what it all meant. We had been liberated. We were free at last. Through the grace of God we had made it. I lit up a cigarette and got drunk. It had been quite awhile since we had any tobacco.

This was the day the war was over. I cannot describe the feeling I felt. Part of me was numb. I thought of my family, they had not heard from me in about four months. They did not know if I was still alive. I was only about half alive at this point. I weighed about ninety-nine pounds. This was May 2, 1945. In less than a month I would be twenty-two years old.

Being liberated meant that we didn't have to march any-more, but that left hundreds of us wandering around the countryside wondering where to go. That afternoon Ed and I kind of came to our senses in a town called Moosburg. We were walking down the street when I saw the rear end of a truck in a garage. I said to Ed, "If we could get that truck, we could get ourselves out of here!" He said, "Let's go." We went into the garage and we didn't see anybody. I got into the truck under the steering wheel and Ed got in on the passenger side. The key was in the ignition and I looked around inside the truck. I saw a round object under my legs. I said to Ed, "Do you think this is a bomb?" "It could be," he said. "Well, let's find out," I said. I closed my eyes and turned the switch.

Well, it wasn't a bomb, because if it were I would not be here today. That thing started up with a roar. I started backing it out of the garage. About this time a man came running out of the house waving his arms and shouting. I stopped the truck and handed him three cigarettes. That's what he got for that truck. Ed and I thought we needed it more than he did. We drove this truck back to the area where we had been liberated and there were still a bunch of ex-POW's everywhere. We told them to load up. We were headed to Holland or Belgium, whichever came first. In about half a minute that truck was loaded. It had a big bed in the back and they were hanging on the running boards, fenders, on top of the cab.

As we started to leave the area we came across some Russian POW's. They had caught Big Stoop. They had tied him behind a truck by his feet and had cut off his head. They were dragging him down the road. I did not feel sorry for him, thinking of what he had done to me and so many others. He got what he deserved.

As we were going down the road with a whole truckload of ex-POW's, we came to a roadblock. It was British. They stopped us and asked where we were going. We told them anywhere but here, but wanted to get to Belgium. He said to wait and came back with two British soldiers. They said we could not go down the road without some kind of escort, as we did not look like American soldiers. We didn't, 86 days on that march without even being able to take a bath. What a sight we were.

Two British soldiers stood on the running boards as our escort. It took us a day and a night to get to Belgium. We unloaded our passengers and started back with the two British escorts. Ed and I made three trips from the liberation area. Each time we had to cross a big river that had a pontoon bridge across it. We were so heavy loaded I thought we would sink the pontoon bridge, but we made it across it. Three times with our load of half-dead men. After the third trip the British would not let us go back. They said we had done enough. I guess we brought nearly one hundred men out.

They took our truck and put us into a building with a lot of showers. We still had on our filthy clothes. We stripped down to our birthday suits and they took a pitchfork and threw our rags out the window, body lice and all. After we took a real hot shower, the first one in about four months, we had to stand in line to get all our body hair sprayed with DDT to kill the body lice. I had made pretty good friends with some of the lice, but I had them long enough. I guess in war you had to say goodbye to all kinds of friends. Thank God they were gone.

After we had ourselves cleaned up they outfitted us with new uniforms. At last we looked like American soldiers again. If you have never lost your freedom, it is impossible to describe how it feels to get it back. For a year I had no control over where I ate, slept, or walked, or what I did. It was a hopeless situation, wondering every minute whether I was going to live or die. The fundamental part of my life was taken away. Freedom is the most important thing we have. I will never lose it again.

Home Again

After a few days with the British, they sent us to LeHavre, France to a place they called Camp Lucky Strike. Ed and I were still together. They were shipping us out as fast as they could to the good ole USA. Before we were to get on a ship for home, I passed out again in the middle of the road. When I came to, Ed was on his way home. I had to stay about thirty days because I had a real bad fever. I never saw or heard from Ed again for a very long time.

I was put on a ship with a bunch of Army Engineers. They were not ex-POW's and as far as I know I was the only POW on board. We came back to New York Harbor a heck of a lot faster than it took me to go overseas; it was about 4 days. I remember coming into the harbor and seeing the Statue of Liberty for the first time in my life. She was the most beautiful woman I had ever seen! I was standing on the rail of the ship watching the tugboats spraying their fire hoses in greeting us home.

When you go to war, home is a place you may never see again. I was almost home. The ship landed, we got off the boat and they took us into a large room where there were a lot of telephones. I tried to call home. I remembered the number for my sister Lillie, but I called Chattanooga, TN, instead of Ringgold, Georgia. I never got through. The next morning they put me on a train headed to Chattanooga, to the Chattanooga Choo Choo train station. This was the same station I left from to go to war four years earlier.

There was no one to meet me, since they didn't know I was coming. As a matter of fact they didn't even know I was back in the USA. When I left for war my mother lived at 2106 South Broad St. That was the only place I knew so I got in a taxi and told him where I wanted to go. It was 4 o'clock in the morning. I told the cab driver about my POW experiences. I asked him how much I owed him, and he said, "Son, you don't owe me nothing, you have already paid your bill. God bless you."

I went to the door of the house where I lived when I left. It was locked. I knocked on the door and a big fat lady came to the door. My mother was a real small woman. Before I thought I said, "Who the hell are you?" She looked at me and said, "Are you the Honeycutt boy?" I said, "Yes, I am." She said I was to go next door, to a two-story house where the Springfield's lived when I left and still did. As I got to the top of the stairs, Mrs. Springfield came out and grabbed me, she was crying because she knew who I was.

She took me inside, handed me a phone and told me to dial a number. I did and my sister Lillie answered it. I choked up – it was perhaps a minute before I could say anything. She kept saying, "Who is this?" I finally blurted out, "Sis, this is Tootsie!" I heard her scream and yell, "It's him!" Lillie and I were always real close. I told her where I was and asked her to come get me. She yelled, "Yes, yes, yes!"

I hung up and waited for her and Charley, my brother-in-law, to come pick me up. It wasn't long before I heard them coming up the stairs, and when my sister got to the top of the stairs she saw me and passed out. I had lost so much weight. In just a few minutes she came to herself, grabbed me and would not turn me loose.

Charley had an old car, I don't know what year it was, but they carried me in it over to Lowery St. where they had moved. It was just cracking day when we got to Mom's house. We knocked on the door and Mom came to answer it. When she opened the door I grabbed her. At the moment she thought I was my brother Edward who was in the service, too. When she finally knew who I was she would not turn me loose. My baby sister, Christine, and my baby brother Raymond were on the bed jumping up and down.

The first things Mom asked me were was I all right and was I hungry. I had the best breakfast of my life that morning. Eggs, ham and good coffee, not burnt acorns, and the best part of it was that I was free and I was home at last. I spent the whole day telling my family all the gruesome things that had happened to me. After that day they never asked me about it again. It was very hard telling it then, and fifty-eight years later it still isn't easy. I came out of the service with post-traumatic stress and to this day I relive it like it is happening all over again.

I had been engaged to a girl that lived on Jefferson St. When I went to see her at her mother's house I found out she was married and four months pregnant. She told me she thought I would not come back. That was the last time I ever saw her. I still wonder what would have happened if she had waited for me.

My older brother, Bug, came home from the Navy. He and I started picking up my lost teenage years. He knew a lot of girls and I think he tried to show me off to all of them. I had a chest full of medals and an arm full of stripes. We had a ball. I had a ninety-day furlough and he and I would go day and night most of the time.

All good things must come to an end, and Bug decided to get married to this girl he was dating and wanted to me to get married, too. It seemed like a good idea at the time. This was in August 1945. I married the girl I was dating the same night Bug got married, and then I went to get my discharge at San Antonio, Texas. I was there a couple of weeks before I got my discharge. They gave me my back pay, which was very little, not enough to get home on. A lot of the ex-soldiers were trying to hitch hike home, and I was one of them, from San Antonio to Chattanooga.

It was not bad to start with as we were still in our uniforms. There were thousands of us on the road trying to get home. Another ex-soldier and I went into a restaurant at 2:00 a.m in a small town in Louisiana. We got a cup of coffee and a donut. While we were eating, a taxi cab driver came over to us and said we could ride out with him to the edge of town. An officer, the soldier, and I got into the cab. We didn't know it at the time, but the driver had been drinking. We found out real soon. In two blocks he was going sixty miles an hour.

There was a military car stopped on the road ahead picking up some soldiers and this cab driver never slowed down. He hit the back of that car going sixty miles an hour. He knocked the military car into the soldiers on the side of the road, killing two of them. The officer in the front seat of the cab went through the windshield. The soldier and I in the back seat were shook up a lot but not hurt too bad. The cab then caught on fire. I had enough fire to last me a lifetime. The soldier and I decided we didn't have any business there, so we left. He went one way and I went another and I wondered if I'd ever get back home.

Just before daybreak I saw a semi-truck coming, I stuck up my thumb and he stopped. He asked me where I was going and I told him Chattanooga. He said that was where he was going, too, and the next thing I knew we were in Chattanooga. I thanked him and have never forgotten his kindness to a soldier trying to get home.

The Rest of the Story

Getting home is sometimes a very hard thing to do. My marriage lasted 24 years and we had two children, Robert Eugene and Robin Annette. There were some difficult things that happened and I decided I had to end the marriage. It wasn't long after this that I met a wonderful girl, whose name was Hazel. I wished I had met her after I got out of the service. We had ten dollars when we got married. I had built and owned several pieces of valuable property but left my first marriage with just the shirt on my back. We made a new life together and I have never regretted it. She has always been there for me; she has been my angel.

Here is an interesting note I cannot explain. The year was 1986. Hazel had to go to the dentist one day and I went with her. She went into the dentist and I sat down to wait for her. I have always loved to read so I reached over and picked up a *Reader's Digest.* I opened the book about halfway. I could not believe my eyes. It was a recruiting ad for the Army showing a black and white photo of a ship with soldiers coming home from World War II. They were all lined up on the railing. There I stood on the railing. It was the ship with the Army Engineers I had come home on. All the memories came flooding into my mind. It had been almost forty years before. When Hazel came out I showed her the book and picture. She could not believe it either.

It was 1989 when someone called me one night and asked me if I was an ex-POW and I said, "Yes, I am." Then he asked me if I had been on the death march with a guy named Ed. I said, yes, and then he said, "I have been looking for you since 1945." It was Ed Follett and he had seen my name in an ex-POW magazine. It was a short time after that we got together. I lived in Ocala, Fla. and he lived in Michigan, and several months later we had a reunion along with Don Kennedy at my home in Florida. We were able to reminisce and fill in many details of what had happened to us. Don Kennedy died not long after that and Ed died in 1992. As far as I know, I am the only survivor of the enlisted men crew of *Hell's Belles*.

Ed and I drawing a map of the death march. We measured around 800 miles.

In June of 2001, I was diagnosed with Stage 3 colon cancer. I was seventy-eight years old. I had colon surgery, chemotherapy and radiation. The chemo had made me so sick, and there was an infection somewhere that they could not find. I stayed in the hospital twenty-four days, four days in intensive care. The surgeon told Hazel that she needed to do an exploratory operation to find out what was wrong and that if she didn't do it I would be gone in a matter of hours. Hazel signed the consent and they took me straight to the operating room. She first explored the original incision where my colon cancer had been. She could not find anything. I had a port in my right shoulder for chemotherapy, and the surgeon told Hazel later that all of a sudden she thought about the port. She took it out and sent it to the lab. What they found in the port was two major types of blood poisoning. She knew then what she had to do and did it. I will never forget what she did for me and Hazel. She saved my life.

I am now eighty years old and Hazel and I have been married thirty-three years. We moved from Florida to a beautiful home in Lookout Mountain, Georgia, where we lived for several years. We have been blessed by family and friends who still stand by us everyday. So far the cancer is gone and hasn't come back and for that I am thankful to the good Lord.

Having cancer is something I think about every day. The statistics say that I have about a twenty- percent chance of being alive in five years. Well, so far I'm still here. I don't know why I have survived so many brushes with death. I do know that I have learned a few things and I want to tell you this:

If it's not your time to go, it's not your time to go. Live your life.

Take care of the people around you.

Never, Never, lose your freedom.

Excerpts from the
CONGRESSIONAL RECORD
PROCEEDINGS AND DEBATES OF 104th CONGRESS,
FIRST SESSION
VOL.141 WASHINGTON, MONDAY MAY 8, 1995
NO.75
SENATE
COMMEMORATING THE 50th ANNIVERSARY
OF THE FORCED MARCH OF AMERICAN
PRISONERS OF WAR FROM STALAG LUFT IV.

Mr. Warner. Mr. President, today we commemorate the 50th anniversary of the end of World War II in Europe. Victory in Europe Day is one of the milestone dates of this century. I rise today to honor a group of Americans who made a large contribution to the allied victory in Europe while also enduring more than their fair share of personal suffering and sacrifice: the brave men who were prisoners of war.

I believe it is appropriate to commemorate our World War II POW's by describing one incident from the war that is emblematic of the unique service rendered by those special people. This is the story of an 86-day ...forced march that commenced at a POW camp known as Stalag Luft IV, near Grosstychow, Poland, on February 6,1945... The ordeal of 9,500 men, most of whom were U.S. Army Air Force Bomber Command Noncommissioned Officers, who suffered through incredible hardships on the march yet survived, stands as an everlasting testimonial to the triumph of the American spirit over immeasurable adversity and of the indomitable ability of camaraderie, teamwork, and fortitude to overcome brutality, horrible conditions, and human suffering.

Bomber crews shot down over axis countries often went through terrifying experiences even before being confined in concentration camps. Flying through withering flak, while also having to fight off enemy fighters, the bomber crews routinely saw other aircraft in formations blown to bits or turned into fiery coffins. Those who were taken POW had to endure their own planes being shot down or otherwise damaged sufficiently to cause the crews to bail out. Often crewmates – close friends – did not make it out of the burning aircraft. Those lucky enough to see their parachutes open, had to then go through a perilous descent amid flak and gunfire from the ground. Many crews were then captured by incensed civilians who had seen their property destroyed or had loved ones killed or maimed by allied bombs. Those civilians at time would beat, spit upon, or even try to lynch the captured crews. And in the case of Stalag Luft IV, once the POW's had arrived at the railroad station near the camp, though exhausted, unfed, and often wounded, many were forced to run the 2 miles to the camp at the point of bayonets. Those who dropped behind were either bayoneted or bitten on the legs by police dogs. And all that was just the prelude to their incarceration where they were underfed, overcrowded, and often maltreated.

In February 1945, the Soviet offensive was rapidly pushing toward Stalag Luft IV. The German high command determined that it was necessary that the POW's be evacuated and moved into Germany. But by that stage of the war, German materiel was at a premium, and neither sufficient railcars nor trucks were available to move prisoners. Therefore the decision was made to move the allied prisoners by foot in forced road march.

...Unfortunately, the story of the men of Stalag Luft IV, replete with tales of the selfless and often heroic deeds of prisoners looking after other prisoners and helping each other to survive under deplorable conditions, is not well known. I therefore rise today to bring their saga of victory over incredible adversity to the attention of my colleagues. I trust that these comments will serve as a springboard for a wider awareness among the American people of what the prisoners from Stalag Luft IV – and all prisoners of war camps – endured in the pursuit of freedom.

Mr. President, I am sure that my colleagues join me in saluting... survivors of Stalag Luft IV March, and all the brave Americans who were prisoners of war in World War II. Their service was twofold: first as fighting men putting their lives on the line, each day, in the cause of freedom and then as prisoners of war, stoically enduring incredible hardships and showing their captors that the American spirit cannot be broken, no matter how terrible the conditions are. We owe them a great debt of gratitude and the memory of their service our undying respect.

John Warner U. S. S.

War medals received by Robert H. Honeycutt

Benghazi rock pit

Two jackasses in Benghazi

*I found it very hard
to drive this truck.*

At the beach in Tel Aviv

Two of my best friends, Jewish soldiers in Tel Aviv

Ready to go on a mission

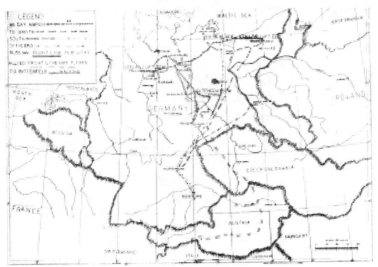

Death March route

Hell's Belles Crew

Back Row L-R:

Leroy Gerber (Don Kennedy substituted)
Edwin R. Follett (Ed)
Frederick Daniels (turret gunner)
Z.V. Penny (Rt waist gunner)
Victor Hawthorne (Lt waist gunner)
George Furdich (tail gunner)

Front Row L-R

Bill Foster (pilot)
Lt. Elder (co-pilot)
Lt. Rochner
Lt. Skopic